The Wild Outdoors

GO BIRDWATCHING!

Julia Garstecki

raintree

Raintree is an imprint of Capstone Global Library Limited, a company incorporated in England and Wales having its registered office at 264 Banbury Road, Oxford, OX2 7DY – Registered company number: 6695582

www.raintree.co.uk
myorders@raintree.co.uk

Hardback edition © Capstone Global Library Limited 2022
Paperback edition © Capstone Global Library Limited 2023
The moral rights of the proprietor have been asserted.

All rights reserved. No part of this publication may be reproduced in any form or by any means (including photocopying or storing it in any medium by electronic means and whether or not transiently or incidentally to some other use of this publication) without the written permission of the copyright owner, except in accordance with the provisions of the Copyright, Designs and Patents Act 1988 or under the terms of a licence issued by the Copyright Licensing Agency, 5th Floor, Shackleton House, 4 Battle Bridge Lane, London SE1 2HX (www.cla.co.uk). Applications for the copyright owner's written permission should be addressed to the publisher.

Edited by Mandy Robbins
Designed by Jennifer Bergstrom
Media research by Morgan Walters
Original illustrations © Capstone Global Library Limited 2022
Originated by Capstone Global Library Ltd
Production by Tori Abraham

978 1 3982 3558 8 (hardback)
978 1 3982 3557 1 (paperback)

British Library Cataloguing in Publication Data
A full catalogue record for this book is available from the British Library.

Acknowledgements
We would like to thank the following for permission to reproduce photographs: Alamy: Pictorial Press Ltd, 27 (bottom); iStockphoto: kali9, 29, robertcicchetti, 21; Shutterstock: 4thebirds, 11, Agami Photo Agency, Cover, Brian A Jackson, 17, (bottom right), Daboost, 17, (bottom left), Danita Delimont, 24, Dennis Jacobsen, 23, Erni, 5, Gregory Johnston, 20, Jakinnboaz, 12, Jessica2, 17, (bottom middle), Lakeview Images, 9, Micah Watson, 27, (top), Michal Ninger, 15, Nadiia Korol, 16, Orla, 7, Pascal De Munck, 14, paula french, 6, Pigprox, 1, Rochelle Rascon, 13, SanderMeertinsPhotography, 8, TerraceStudio, 17, (top), Victor Suarez Naranjo, 19, WaceQ, 22

All the internet addresses (URLs) given in this book were valid at the time of going to press. However, due to the dynamic nature of the internet, some addresses may have changed, or sites may have changed or ceased to exist since publication. While the author and publisher regret any inconvenience this may cause readers, no responsibility for any such changes can be accepted by either the author or the publisher.

Printed and bound in India.

Contents

Chapter 1
CALL OF THE WILD.. 4

Chapter 2
EARLY BIRD OR NIGHT OWL?........................... 8

Chapter 3
LET'S GO BIRDWATCHING!................................10

Chapter 4
WHERE TO FIND YOUR FEATHERED FRIENDS.........18

Chapter 5
NEXT-LEVEL BIRDWATCHING............................... 26

    Glossary 30
    Find out more 31
    Index 32

Chapter 1

CALL OF THE WILD

You stand beside a tree, quiet as can be. Sun rays sparkle on the surface of a lake. Some of your friends flick through their **field guides**. Others point to a tree. A large nest made of sticks rests high at the top. This is the spot! You wait.

A noise comes from above. You look towards the sound. The bird flying overhead is more beautiful and majestic than any photos you've seen. The osprey flaps its enormous wings. It soars gracefully over the lake, looking for food. You cannot take your eyes off it. The osprey suddenly dives and grabs a fish from the water. It soars up and away. This rare sight was definitely worth the wait.

An osprey catching a fish

FACT

There are about 8,850 different kinds of birds in the world today.

Birdwatching is a popular hobby. It is an activity that anyone can do, because birds are everywhere. And it's a low-cost hobby that gets you outside, which is good for your health. More people are discovering that birdwatching is entertaining, relaxing and can leave you feeling more connected to nature.

There are thousands of different kinds of birds to seek out. Ostriches in Africa look completely different from the penguins of Antarctica. Penguins look completely different from the white-headed Reeves pheasants of China.

An ostrich

Birds behave as differently as they look. Certain cockatoos hit twigs against trees and make music. Flamingoes eat with their heads upside-down. Some thrushes fart to move leaves in search of worms. Birdwatching is the perfect way to spy on these intelligent and fascinating animals.

Ancient ancestors

Have you ever thought that chickens looked like dinosaurs? Chickens and ostriches are the closest living things to dinosaurs. They are related to theropods. This group of dinosaurs included the Tyrannosaurus rex. Some theropods could fly. Over millions of years, these flying dinosaurs **evolved** into the chickens you see today.

A Tyrannosaurus rex

Chapter 2
EARLY BIRD OR NIGHT OWL?

The time of day you go birdwatching matters. No matter where you are, you can see different birds at different times of the day. Have you heard the saying "The early bird catches the worm"? Many birds are active at sunrise. That is when many insects are on the move. These creatures are often breakfast for a bird!

Eurasian reed warbler

Not all birds are early birds. Hawks are more active during the warmer parts of the day. If you want to see them, go out in the afternoon. And if you like to stay up late, you might be called a "night owl". This is because most owls hunt at night. Whether you are birdwatching at sunrise or sunset, in the town or at a lake, your chances of seeing birds are excellent.

The morepork, New Zealand's native owl

The more you travel, the more kinds of birds you'll see. Some birds, such as pigeons, live well in cities but also live on rocky cliffs. Other birds, such as ducks and herons, prefer water.

FACT

Not all owls are active at night and sleep during the day. The northern hawk owl and the northern pygmy owl sleep at night and are active during the day.

Chapter 3

LET'S GO BIRDWATCHING!

You can go birdwatching anywhere at any time. But how will you know what you are looking at? A field guide will help you. A field guide is a book used to identify different kinds of birds. Field guides can be organized by bird size and shape or location.

Before birdwatching, look through your field guide. Is there a particular bird you want to see? A field guide will tell you where you have the best chances of seeing it. For example, house martins can be spotted in the UK between the months of April and September, then they fly to Africa for the winter.

You can compare the photos of birds in your field guide to those you see in nature.

Parts of a bird

When you go birdwatching, take a field guide and a trusted adult with you. **Observe** the birds. Notice the **markings** on different parts of their bodies. All birds have special markings on different parts of their bodies. The tip of the bird's head is the crown. Under the beak is the throat. Below that is the breast of the bird. There may be markings on the back, wings and tail of the bird as well.

If you find a nest with eggs, mark the location. Then you can come back and watch the young birds hatch and grow up. But be careful not to disturb the nest or birds.

Along with your field guide, bring a pen and a notebook to keep notes. A camera is a great idea as well. Then, once your feathered friend has gone away, look back at your notes or photos. You can refer to the field guide to identify the bird.

Never disturb birds' eggs. You can observe from a distance.

A hummingbird sips nectar from a flower.

There are things you can do to improve your chances of seeing more birds. First, stay quiet. Noise will scare birds away. You might be surprised at how much you hear once you are silent. Birds will start to hop or sing. Woodpeckers will tap on the trees.

Look carefully. Where would a bird **perch** or hide? Look at tree branches, bushes or a shoreline. Clumps of leaves or twigs might be a nest. Also, keep an eye on the sky. Which way are birds flying? Where did they come from? Good birdwatchers are observant and patient. The more you practise, the better trained you will be for noticing birds.

Once you've been birdwatching a few times, you will notice things you may not have noticed before. For example, see how different birds' beaks are shaped.

Duck beaks, more commonly called bills, are long and spoon shaped. Bills crush food in the same way our teeth chew. The shape of a duck's bill is perfect for separating food from water.

The hummingbird's beak is long and narrow. It protects the bird's long tongue as it laps up **nectar** and water.

Woodpeckers have long, pointed beaks. They are perfect for drilling into trees. Woodpeckers use their beaks to look for insects to eat.

A woodpecker pecks for insects in a tree trunk.

Binoculars are helpful when birdwatching. Then you can watch a bird from afar without disturbing it. A light pair of binoculars is best. If you go birdwatching for several hours, a light pair is easier to carry.

If you have a smartphone, download some birdwatching apps. Apps such as Birds of Britain or the Collins British Bird Guide can help identify the birds you see. You could also take a photo of the bird and upload it on the app to identify it.

You can listen to bird songs on the app as well. Compare the app sounds to the bird you have heard. Soon, you will know the call of a blue tit, the screech of an osprey, or the hoot of an owl. Do not play bird songs while you are out birdwatching, though!

BIROWATCHING PACK LIST

- ☑ field guide
- ☑ binoculars
- ☑ weather-appropriate clothing
- ☑ camera/smartphone
- ☑ notebook and pens
- ☑ sturdy shoes
- ☑ sunscreen
- ☑ insect repellent
- ☑ hat

Chapter 4
WHERE TO FIND YOUR FEATHERED FRIENDS

Birdwatching in the city can be very exciting! Pigeons, house sparrows and starlings live well in cities. But larger birds live in cities too. Berlin, Germany, is home to large populations of goshawks. These hawks feed on wild pigeons and rats. In fact, if you see pigeons anywhere, goshawks are likely to be near by.

Kites are a type of bird of prey that build their nests in trees in Delhi, India. Like goshawks, they feed on smaller birds and rats. Kites even help clean the rubbish off the streets! Many birdwatchers have begun studying **urban** birds like kites. They study how birds and people can help each other.

A black kite in Dehli, India

There are many birds to be seen in the larger cities of South Africa. In the Cape Town area, yellow-billed egrets, kingfishers and Cape sugarbirds can be found.

FACT

Male birds tend to be more colourful than females. This is because they need to attract a female mate.

A blue heron soars through the air.

Water sources are a great place to go birdwatching. One popular type of water bird is the heron. Herons are found almost anywhere there is water. Birdwatchers in Europe, North America, Asia, Africa and Australia can study these long-legged beauties as they hunt in shallow waters. Once you spot one, watch as it hunts. Stay to watch it fly off. Herons look as if they are flying in slow motion.

Where there is water, there will probably be ducks. Ducks are great for beginner birdwatchers to observe. **Dabblers** are ducks that feed with their back ends in the air. A mallard is a type of dabbler. Other ducks are diving ducks. They include the tufted duck and the pochard. They dive deep into the water. Eiders are the largest ducks in the Northern Hemisphere. They spend much of their time in icy Arctic waters.

Pale Male

Pale Male is one of the most famous red-tailed hawks of all time. He moved to Fifth Avenue in New York City, USA, in about 1991. Pale Male made his nest in Central Park. Bird watchers called him that because of his uncommonly light-coloured feathers. The dozens of red-tailed hawks spotted around the city are probably his children or grandchildren.

A red-tailed hawk in Central Park

A robin perches on a branch.

When birdwatching in **rural** areas, you are likely to come across blackbirds. Other common birds found in many areas include robins, blue tits, starlings and chaffinches. You are more likely to hear these birds before you see them. Be still and listen carefully!

Experienced birdwatchers know tips to spot more birds. First, keep the sun behind you. This way birds will not appear shadowed. Not only will they be easier to see, but you'll get a better view of the birds' colours. Another trick good birdwatchers use is called pishing. Pishing is when a birdwatcher makes small kissing noises. It's quiet enough that the birds don't get scared, but they do get curious and want to explore the sound.

Blue tits can be often be seen in gardens and parks.

Birds gather in a garden to eat seeds from a bird feeder.

There may be times when an adult isn't able to take you birdwatching. But you can still bring the birds to you! Different kinds of bird feeders attract different kinds of birds.

If you live in a city, an in-house window feeder is a good option. This plastic feeder sits on the windowsill. Rather than hanging outside your window, it actually curves into the house! You can also find bird feeders with suction cups that stick outside your windows. Once birds get comfortable with your bird feeder, you are likely to have regular visitors.

Different types of birds like different types of food. Robins, blackbirds, starlings and blue tits like mealworms. Jays, jackdaws, crows and magpies prefer peanuts. Sparrows, dunnocks and finches like seeds. If you hang a feeder tube filled with niger seeds in your garden, you may see some goldfinches.

It can take some time for birds to find a new feeder. Birdwatching takes patience sometimes, but it's worth the excitement when the birds come to visit.

Chapter 5
NEXT-LEVEL BIRDWATCHING

Birdwatching is a growing hobby. Many parks and schools have bird-watching clubs. One of the best groups that teaches people about birdwatching is the Royal Society for the Protection of Birds (RSPB). This national organization works to protect birds and teaches people about the birds in their area. They have wildlife reserves all round the country that you can visit. Also, their website has lots of information about how to spot birds and how you can help protect them.

BirdLife International is another group trying to help birds. It has branches in more than 100 countries. The group's goal is to **conserve** birds and their **habitats**. Birdwatchers all over the world help BirdLife track bird populations. They learn what helps and harms birds. Then they can teach others what they know.

Emily Williamson

Emily Williamson: inspiring others

In 1889, there was a fashion craze for wearing hats with not just feathers in but also wings and sometimes whole birds. This craze was driving birds such as egrets, great-crested grebes and some birds of paradise towards extinction. Emily Williamson wanted to put a stop to this. She asked other women in her area to assemble and sign a pledge to "Wear No Feathers". They formed the Society for the Protection of Birds. By 1893, the movement had over 10,000 members. In 1904, the society was awarded a Royal Charter, making it the Royal Society for the Protection of Birds.

Being a birdwatcher is a responsibility. It's important to practise good birdwatching habits. Never cause damage to a bird habitat. If you are lucky enough to see eggs in a nest or baby birds, leave them alone. Also, bear in mind that a parent bird might be waiting to come back to the nest to feed her babies. You might be scaring them away.

If you hang up bird feeders, keep them clean. Hang them where it will be safest for birds. A metre or so away from trees or bushes is a good spot. The birds can quickly fly back to the tree if they get scared.

Birdwatching is a rewarding hobby that can be done by anyone, anywhere. The more we watch the birds, the more we notice other aspects of nature. Because birdwatching can help us feel more connected to nature, the hobby inspires many of us to protect it. The more we can keep the environment safe for birds, the more birds we'll have to enjoy.

GLOSSARY

conserve save

dabbler duck that dabs its head underwater to trap food

evolve when a type of animal changes slowly over time to adapt better to its environment

field guide book for the identification of birds, flowers, minerals or other things in their natural environment

habitat natural place and conditions in which a plant or animal lives

marking patch of colour or pattern of marks on fur, feathers or skin

nectar sweet liquid found in many flowers

observe watch someone or something closely in order to learn something

perch when a bird finds a high place where it can rest and view its surroundings

rural of the countryside; away from cities and towns

urban having to do with a city, town or built-up area

FIND OUT MORE

BOOKS

Birds of the British Isles (Let's Look At), Lucy Beevor (Raintree, 2019)

Out and About Bird Spotter: A Children's Guide to Over 100 Different Birds, Robyn Swift (Nosy Crow, 2019)

The Big Book of Birds, Yuval Zommer (Thames & Hudson, 2019)

WEBSITES

www.dkfindout.com/uk/animals-and-nature/birds/
The DKFindout! website has facts on many different types of birds.

www.rspb.org.uk/birds-and-wildlife/wildlife-guides/identify-a-bird/
If you're not sure which type of bird you have spotted, look it up on the RSPB bird identifier.

INDEX

apps 16–17
    Birds of Britain 16
    Collins British Bird
      Guide 16
bald eagles 4, 5
binoculars 16, 17
bird feeders 25, 28
BirdLife International 26
blue tits 17, 22, 25

Cape sugarbirds 19
chaffinch 22
cockatoos 7

ducks 9, 15, 21
dunnocks 25

eggs 13, 28
Eurasian reed warblers 8

field guides 4, 10, 11, 12,
   13, 17
flamingoes 7

goldfinches 24, 25

hawks 8
    goshawks 18
    red-tailed hawks,
      Pale Male 21
herons 9, 20

house martins 10
hummingbirds 14, 15, 25

kingfishers 19
kites 18, 19

markings 12

nests 4, 13, 14, 21, 28

orioles 25
ospreys 17
ostriches 6, 7
owls 8, 9, 17

penguins 6
pigeons 9, 18
pishing 23

robins 13, 22
Royal Society for the Protection
   of Birds (RSPB) 26-27

sparrows 18, 24
starlings 18, 22

thrushes 7

Williamson, Emily 27

woodpeckers 14, 15, 22

yellow-billed egrets 19